Moonbook and Sunbook

OTHER BOOKS BY WILLIS BARNSTONE

Poetry

Poems of Exchange
From This White Island
Antijournal
A Day in the Country
New Faces of China
China Poems
Overheard
A Snow Salmon Reached the Andes Lake
Ten Gospels and a Nightingale
The Alphabet of Night
Five A.M. in Beijing
Funny Ways of Staying Alive
The Secret Reader: 501 Sonnets
Algebra of Night: New & Selected Poems 1948–1998
Life Watch
Café de l'Aube à Paris / Dawn Café in Paris
Stickball on 88th Street
ABC of Translation: Poems & Drawings

Translations

Eighty Poems of Antonio Machado
The Other Alexander, novel by Margarita Liberaki (with Helle Barnstone)
Greek Lyric Poetry
Physiologus Theobaldli Episcopi … (Bishop Theobald's Bestiary)
Sappho: Poems in the Original Greek with a Translation
The Poems of Saint John of the Cross
The Song of Songs: Shir Hashirim
The Poems of Mao Zedong
My Voice Because of You, poems by Pedro Salinas
The Unknown Light: The Poems of Fray Luis de León
A Bird of Paper: Poems of Vicente Aleixandre (with David Garrison)
Laughing Lost in the Mountains: Poems of Wang Wei (with Tony Barnstone
    and Xu Haixin)
Six Masters of the Spanish Sonnet
To Touch the Sky: Poems of Mystical, Spiritual and Metaphysical Light

Sonnets to Orpheus, poems by Rainer Maria Rilke
Border of a Dream: Selected Poems of Antonio Machado
The Complete Poems of Sappho
Ancient Greek Lyrics
Love Poems of Pedro Salinas

Memoir

With Borges on an Ordinary Evening in Buenos Aires
Sunday Morning in Fascist Spain: A European Memoir, 1948–1953
We Jews and Blacks: Memoir with Poems (with Yusef Komunyakaa)

Literary Criticism

The Poetics of Ecstasy: From Sappho to Borges
The Poetics of Translation: History, Theory, and Practice

Biblical

The Other Bible: Ancient Alternative Scriptures
The New Covenant: Four Gospels and Apocalypse
The Restored New Testament, Including the Gnostic Gospels …
The Poems of Jesus Christ
The Gnostic Bible (with Marvin Meyer)
Essential Gnostic Scriptures (with Marvin Meyer)
Masterpieces of Gnostic Wisdom (compact disc, with Marvin Meyer)

Anthologies/Editions

Modern European Poetry: French, Spanish, Russian, Greek, Italian, German
Spanish Poetry from Its Beginnings through the Nineteenth Century
Rinconete and Cortadillo, by Miguel de Cervantes (with Hugh Carter)
Eighteen Texts: Writings by Contemporary Greek Authors
Concrete Poetry: A World View (with Mary Ellen Solt)
A Book of Women Poets from Antiquity to Now (with Aliki Barnstone)
Borges at 80: Conversations
Literatures of Asia, Africa, and Latin America (with Tony Barnstone)
Literatures of the Middle East (with Tony Barnstone)
Literatures of Latin America

MOONBOOK *and* SUNBOOK

Willis Barnstone

Tupelo Press
North Adams, Massachusetts

Moonbook and Sunbook.
Poems and drawings copyright 2014 Willis Barnstone. All rights reserved.

Library of Congress Cataloging-in-Publication Data
Barnstone, Willis, 1927–   author.
[Poems. Selections]
Moonbook and Sunbook / Willis Barnstone. -- First paperback edition.
    pages cm
ISBN 978-1-936797-46-2 (hardcover : alk. paper) -- ISBN 978-1-936797-42-4
(pbk. : alk. paper)
I. Title.
PS3552.A722A6 2014
811'.54--dc23

                                        2014002561

Cover and text designed by Bill Kuch.

First edition: April 2014.

Tupelo Press
P.O. Box 1767, North Adams, Massachusetts 01247
Telephone: (413) 664–9611 / editor@tupelopress.org
www.tupelopress.org

Tupelo Press is an award-winning independent literary press that publishes fine
fiction, nonfiction, and poetry in books that are a joy to hold as well as read.
Tupelo Press is a registered 501(c)3 non-profit organization, and we rely on public
support to carry out our mission of publishing extraordinary work that may be
outside the realm of large commercial publishers. Financial donations are welcome
and are tax deductible.

for my father Robert Barnstone born in Boston
where I wrote this book for him

Contents

MOONBOOK

SUNBOOK

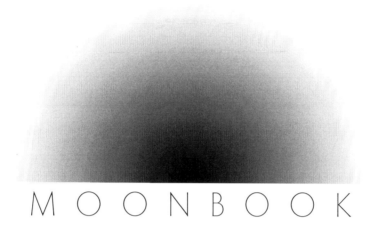

MOONBOOK

The

Good

Beasts

The Good Beasts

On the first morning of the moon, in land
under the birds of Ur, before the flood
dirties the memory of a couple banned
from apples and the fatal fire of blood,
Adam and Eve walk in the ghetto park,
circling a tree. They do not know the way
to make their bodies shiver in the spark
of fusion, cannot read or talk, and they
know night and noon, but not the enduring night
of nights that has no noon. Adam and Eve,
good beasts, living the morning of the globe,
are blind, like us, to apocalypse. They probe
the sun, death ray, on the red tree. Its light
rages, illiterate, until they leave.

Gospel of Clouds

On cloudy Sundays clouds are in my heart
as if my brother came, as if the rain
lingered among the mushrooms and the art
of freedom washed into the murder train
or rinsed the peat bog soldiers of the camp.[1]
On cloudy Sundays clouds are with Joe Hill.
Last night I dreamt he was alive. The tramp
was mining clouds for thunder. And uphill
into the clouds I feel that time descends,
as if my mother came, as if the moon
were flowering between the thighs of friends
and gave us fire. On Sundays when the swan
of death circles my heart, the cloudy noon
rolls me gaping like dice, though I am gone.

[1] Notes indicated by superscript will be found at the back of the book.

Chatting with Half Moon

These woods are green, alive, but have no mind
like the black sun dancing on broken toes.
This half moon's not alive, though she is kind
for a dead woman. She's my wife. She knows
nothing of me, yet sneaks me light. I take
her love, and every night I search her face,
her stony aphrodisiac hips, and stake
my emptiness on her. She rolls in place
since she checked out from earth. In our few years
we both are aching terribly alone.
I talk to her mirror face, her cold glass,
and love her naturally, and have no fears
for her existence. "Though I am mere bone,"
she whispers, "Come. Join my luminous mass."

Moon Dropping into Our Secret Dutch Attic, 1943

I want to be useful or bring enjoyment to all people,
even those I've never met.
—Anne Frank

Moon, you catch oceans, glitter them with sun
you flash out from your face, but I am down
here and see just these attic rays. No one
to slip me from this room. You coat each town
with brilliance, but you keep your body clean,
untouched by smoking death camps far below
your gaze. When you are thin, a safety pin
of sexual light, I grab your beams and sew
them in my pockets. I Anne find a hole
through the closed shutters in my attic. When
night locks me in, I see your drop of bread
and turn it into ink, and your dead soul
is mine. Your brilliance through my oxygen
gives me light hope, before I join the dead.

In Málaga a Poet of Moon and Sun

Solomon Ibn Gabirol (1021–c.1055)

Eleventh century in southern Spain,
a Jew scrawls a green poem, talks Arabic
in the white sun. No wind. With ink of rain
and lightning quill he storms the moon. Then quick
as his dream lover's thighs of fire, he drops
down from the scarlet night to sun and white
adobe walls. Gabirol paints the crops
of lime and olive trees in Hebrew light
of old Jerusalem. Yet why scrawl in
that fossil tongue? For God who paints the soul
with glyphs? Solomon Ibn Gabirol
scribbles to make beauty. All poets do.
Happy, cantankerous, he shares our sin
of writing for himself, for God and you.

Silent Friend of Many Distances

The problem with an orange tree in Greece
whose perfume fills the straits between Poros
and hugging Peloponessos is peace
of beauty—radiating always close—
that never can respond but does its part,
issuing hope to make me live and wreak
me zero blind. The problem with the heart,
a tool of time, is want can never speak.
The problem with the brain is darkness. It
has no inner moon lamp to give it place.
Silent rotating friend, your aloof poise
I love and hate. Like every love, far space
creates intensity, yet rains its spit
on us. I rant until I hear your voice.

Goya's Moon

"Yard with Madmen," 1793–1794

Francisco Goya's little yard with madmen
lives in gloom under a yellow sky.
The caretaker horsewhips the naked sad
embracing lunatics. Moons in their eye.
Goya by now is deaf. The men are globs
of paint and lack the balance to conceal
an insane moon in all of us. Their throbs
and inner gales derange their eyes and steal
their right to live outside the yard and wall.
Goya is free. He breaks all rules and saves
us from illusions that we might be sane.
Mad Goya paints the truth of fear, the ball
of hope that soars into the clouds and raves
and falls on fire into his moon-fat brain.

Federico García Lorca

No
one knew and understood
the moon like you, Federico.
She was your child, lover, death. No one could
save you. They lied to Rosales. Falla came
too late. They plugged an extra bullet in your ass
for being a queer who liked strong women, flame
of a dark night of love—*la noche oscura de amor,* the grass
of Andalusia where the tiny John of the Cross soared
from meditation, as a woman, to be one
with God his lord, lover, male whore
and lily moon. Good Federico
dies for the abused moon and sun,
¡NO!

Blue Shirt Firing Squad Fells the Andalusian Poet

In Andalusia sun wears orange sheets of light
    hanging fresh in the woods, but where
is the mare on the sky? Must it be night
    for moon to glow? By day she's there,
a sexual memory in Granada, Spain,
    for green wind Federico. No,
she is a tombstone where the Blue Shirt Cain
firing squad fells him. An ice rainbow
    washes his dawn. And while a cow
lumbers on sky grass, devours a lunar feast
    of plants of green felicity,
while a poppy sighs and a spinning beast
    and child float in his theater, now
the Spaniard's moon of pain torments the sea.

Spanish Moon in Almuñécar, 1951

Behind our Roman aqueduct back wall
at three a.m., the moon like a yellow
buffoon sings over the gray hills and all
the sugarcane is shining in the campo.
Quinces and mother-of-pearl olive groves
fragrant the clouds. I smell mint and spikenard.
The full moon is dashing up the sky, her glow
is chasing carbines of the Civil Guard.
Moon lights the song trembling behind her eyes.
In a girl's voice, like Homer she sings blind:
Mira, mira la lunita, con su carita empelvá.
Guards drape killed bodies on the mules. Sick mind
of the Caudillo's fascist years is a
black moon of executions and Church lies.

Only a Paper Moon in Argentina During the Dirty War

Mario and I talk ourselves blue. Guns talk
in Buenos Aires. Mario Kabbalah.
Dirty War. After his lecture we walk
to the Saint James Café with algebra
of mystic John of the Cross. Mario skips through
the numbers. Jesus calls in Galilee
to turn the waters into doves; the Jew
performs his miracles. It is only
a paper moon outside but witness of
the plateless Ford that rounds up seven men
and throws a woman in its trunk. I hear
the woman shriek. No one can help. No love
of miracle or numbers helps. Again
the paper moon observes the disappeared.

With Borges at the Saint James Café, 1975

We take our favorite spot below the mirror
and waning half moon, cold Araucan bowl
holding a sphere of sunlight for the scholar
and insomniac. Earlier in our stroll
from Calle de Maipú to our café,
we hear the nightly bombs. "We were an honorable
city of humble people, and they
survived on courage. All that is gone
with leaders who've gone mad. I'm sad and yet
I still believe in the nation precisely
because it is a chaos." When we sat
the waiter brought us our hot chocolate
and toast. "You love Milton, don't you? Well, he
too had the gift of blindness and liked to chat."

Wang Wei in Deep South Mountain

In Deep South Mountain, Wang Wei sleeps alone,
recalling his lost wife. The woodcutter in the wood
laughs with him about the moon of stone
glittering on these two bald heads of childhood
friends. When a wandering monk comes for the night,
carrying his books, moon cookies, and a jar
of honey, they talk Buddha light
and joke about how far
their years of exile in the Gobi
touch their poems. They are the only ones
alive in China and forget the moon sees
everything: the cane gate of their adobe
hut, dazed lovers, executed sons,
and two old monks in hermit reverie.

Wang Wei and the Snow

Although Wang Wei is peaceful looking at
the apricot, the moon gull and the frost
climbing the village hills, or feels the mat
of pine trees on the mountain sky, or lost
in meditation loses nature and
the outer light to sing his way through mist
inside—although Wang Wei becomes the land
and loitering rain, his mountain clouds exist
as refugees from thought and turn like mills
never exhausting time. Wang Wei also
is stuck in life, and from his hermitage
he tells a friend to walk the idle hills
alone, to swallow failure like the age-
ing year to dream (what else is there?) of snow.

Li Bai and the Sailor Moon

My comfort's in the windy moon too bright
for sleep. Finally, dead drunk I lie down on
the naked mountain, dreaming I can write
my sorrow on the pillow of the dawn.
Although I freeze under the snow that fell
like egrets floating in the water of
this sleep, my sadness like a white gazelle
wakes by the lake. I'm ruined. I call to love.
I've heard her whisper several times and feel
no shame for indiscretions. Since my wife
is hungry, I have sold my goods and kneel
below the mulberry tree, taking my knife
to cut my shadow from the dock. To home
I row. The sailor moon rolls while I roam.

Li Qingzhao and Her Ink Moon

Reading the lonely poems of Li Qingzhao,
seeing her lying drunk, her hairpins on
the courtyard table as she mourns the bamboo
bed empty of her legal lover, gone
beyond the sky and her apricot tree,
I know those geese and bugles that explode
her evening in the late Song dynasty
signal her unique sorrow on the road
of the blue lotus. By the Eastern Wall
her lord and friend fell into mist. Yet in
that same small garden of their scholar's house
they shared a passion for old scrolls, and when
he went (turning her moon to ink), in all
the world her grieving happened only once.

Burmese Nun Moon

At twilight a horizon nun
glides about in chamomile robes
of clouds over the morose sun.
The new moon in the east disrobes,
a naked Burmese woman thin
amid the planet's icy bloom
of stars. She's wonder in her skin
of light. Within her virgin womb
she holds the full moon she will be.
Her adolescent face is always
an astonishment. To know
is innocence, an ecstasy
of going elsewhere. She is tall
in hope. Her breasts will bloom with snow.

Moon Over a Burmese Graveyard

The moon's discreet, dances for anyone,
but she is intimate with Mozart when
he plays a rondo, taking her night sun
to glow rapturous sky meadows, and then
fill a small room in hidden space. An ear
with light. Salah, carrying a Song jar
of beams she bought in a Rangoon bazaar,
stumbles in northern Burma. No one near
to help. She's in a graveyard. The monsoon
slaps rain down on her grandfather's stone face
eternity has eaten up. The chalky moon
has heart for the courageous lost who speak
her tongue. They suffer solitude. Her space
feeds her bright cosmos to the gentle weak.

Half Moon in Her Choker of Stars, 1949

When I am very young, walking in Greece
on Mount Penteli, I see a half moon
in her choker of stars. Athens police
has her dossier: *She wakes in afternoon
under cover of day. By nigh t she helps
guerrillas burn the hills.* I'm also on
their list of suspects. When the owl yelps
into the clouds, I'm getting laid, half gone,
I think, and want to know her other side
which is the half I'm living now. She still
excites me, though the war in Greece is not
on fire. The moon wants peace. The war I hide
in me. The half moon stays in mist until
she comes out dancing like a rocking yacht.

A Whiff of the Full Moon

The full moon is like now, a flash between
her forms. But we are always trapped in now
except when death croaks all time, wiping clean
absurd eternity. I wonder how
to seize a second of the full moon? No
one can. Full moon's a daffy human, for
she won't be fixed and moves like life. I know
her, nonetheless. I walk along the shore
with her in Greece. Artemis carries her
like a glittering cheese disk over the peaks
of Crete and deer chew her grass scent. I grew
and sank with her. One evening happier
than a blue bowl of basil, I fall weak
into her obscure light and hear her dew.

The Kasbah Moon Can Never Know, 1952

The moon can never know she is the moon,
nor sun know he is sun. The minaret
is deaf, the muezzin yells, the faithful swoon
inside the Tangier mosque, and yet
I talk to her, a blue scimitar in
the sharp kef mist smelling over the city.
I am young in these Kasbah days. My sin
is deep as smiling whores, but don't pity
any Billy. He's stressed, but doesn't know
remorse. Can the moon feel guilt? No,
she's faithful and she never lets me down,
and though far, dumb, a body of dead stone,
I love and crave her. She is beautiful
and her kohl-painted eyelid fills me full.

Lovely French Countess Guillemette in Tangier's Kasbah

The most thrilling moon is in the Kasbah.
I make my oatmeal supper on the gas
burner. Then sleep. Rats in my shoes are ga-
ga, sleeping till the dawn muezzin jazz
fills the neighborhood sky with calls to prayer.
I get up with the rats and swallows in
the roof, and roam through kef down the sun-glare
coast of Africa. Tangier knows no sin.
My French countess asks me to go for tea
and lavish cakes at a Berber's retreat.
"Are you with Christ?" she pops. "No, I'm a Jew."
"You killed our lord!" "No way! He's a Jew too."
"Never heard that before." Suddenly,
the glad moon floods us kissing in the street.

Companion Moon in a Mexican Graveyard, 1945

She is a ball. I like to go on dates
with her. I'm a young squirt. She has no age.
In Miacatlán we are three village mates
lying by blue ceramic graves. But sage
and bright, she doesn't kick up a storm
at our ménage à trois. We hug. She tattoos
romantic light across our chests. Our form,
the two-backed beast of love, is new
to us. Round, trembling, our sweet milk and sweat
grow brilliant as we shake the world away
and come to secret knowing. In Mexico
a graveyard is a private place. We let
night's mercy govern us in moon shadow
by Nahua tombs, collapsing in one ray.

On the Marble Moon

The sun lies on her chalky marble when
I step on her. Too late for me to blast
up like an astronaut. The moon is ten-
der with my secrecy. She sees me cast
away all sense and safety for a walk
on her. I hike inside her lakes. The tears
of seas are gone. Lonely, I try to talk
with her. My wolf dog barks, the moon's thin ears
receive us as if Bach were singing for
his Lord. Her hilly breasts are everywhere
and generous. Blackness expands in me,
a vast peace like a burning moth. Her floor,
the belly of the sky, strips me with care.
I sleep on her horizon. One nude tree.

Poètes dans la lune[2]

Le soleil sans mots lance la lumière
qui éclaire le suave air et la chaleur
pour Eve et Adam. Puis tremblant de peur
ils jouissent en fabriquant nos pères
et meurent. Mais les poètes qu'on aime
dans la lune, je les entends sous l'arche
d'un obscur brouillard sauvage où ils sèment
mon âme avec la douce nuit qui marche.

Poets in the Moon

The wordless sun launches a light
flaring out with delicious air and heat
for Eve and Adam. Shivering with fright,
they love procreating our ancestry,
and die. Yet those poets whom I feed
on in the moon, I hear below the arch
of a somberly wild fog where they seed
the soul with a sweet night on its march.

Working on Talks Around Midnight

Around midnight the bombs cease. A small plane
drops drugged prisoners into the Paraná
The moon engraves the river with a chain
of glittering limbs. Around the table a
few candles light us. Borges, being blind,
needs no bright fires. Outside he has a cane,
but stumbling though his cluttered flat he winds
like deer through trees. "López Rega is insane,"
he mutters. "El brujo."³ "Okay, let's make up
the titles for my talks. All my old friends
are shades," Borges complains. "Yes I am old.
Those friends I grieve, not age." Into his cup
I pour warm wine." "No," he says, so I unfold
chocolate. He eats. "Now my nightmares will end."

A Warm Nun in Her Airless Sphere

The moon is there,
whether or not I peer
at her ice mountain
eyeball. A nun

in her airless sphere,
she is convent cool yet warm.
She astonishes. We're
a never-jaded pair.

I take her arm
in black woods or a city
alley. We talk.

She reads me her poem.
I clap, hug her light. We
chuckle and walk.

Full Moon with Her Lion Eye

The full moon, cold white lion over the forest line,
    yawns weary of eternity, but I freeze
under her rising jaw fresh on my spine.
    My clothes shiver. In them I've gone
a week to Puerto Ayacucho in the Amazonas where
    naked Yanomami watch the tundra swan
fly overhead. She is their hot full moon. They cook
    a baby monkey in a big pot of boiling
water, ask me to share a bowl, I demur, turn north,
    the snow lion always overhead. Empty
of soul, a future of bones, I look at the white beast
    of stone moon with its stone eye on me
for another vagabond week. I plane north for
    the dwarf forest island of St. Pierre,
drink winter brandy with a fat Portuguese sailor,
    dive from his cod boat into the icy hole
of the profligate North Atlantic. João laughs. I drop
    down like craps longing for another roll.

Cheetah Moon in Kenya

A few sleepy cheetahs
on the scrub savannah

in solitary night
amid acacia thorn trees

are stalking me
below the leftover moon

before the orange
explosion of daybreak.

Easter Island Moons in Caves, 1976

All the heavens are nuts with roaring stars
over Easter Island, desolately
drunk for New Year's Eve. Chileans fill the bars.
Eduardo fears he wed. Who might she be?
These archeologists have little work.
With money to restore, they whore and smoke
in Paradise where Pierre Loti berserk
with joy, painted the natives Captain Cook
had used for target practice. Lovely island,
thousands of wild stallions. Living in caves
the naked islanders, noble and mild,
didn't beef. Eduardo forgot to shave.
Some day islanders will bloom. Moons comfort
the poor and sick romantics bless this port.

The Moon Has Poppies in Her Mouth

The moon has poppies in her mouth
and hippos in her lungs. She glows
in Indiana. In the south
of Europe, wrestler Plato knows
that music lends the cosmos soul.
Moon hills cry silence. I invent
her wordless tune. In bed I roll
and roll, seeking the moon who lent
me unheard song. A zoo of ears
on earth listens while silence sings.
Our earthly makers Cole Porter
and Ravel swoon in reverie,
Johannes Brahms in ecstasy.
The mute moon flaps her angel wings.

Priests Are Nailing Her in Place

The moon is sick. I fear she'll die
    from lack of love, from poverty
    and homelessness. Lost in the sky

our daughter's dropping down the sea
    of negligence. And who will glow
    on walkers in the night? The moon

will show and nobody will know
    because she is a black balloon
    and can't be seen. She hasn't gone.

Yet scholars say, "She went. She was
    an obscure custom of a race
    of fools." The moon is sick, and on

her crackled face, a pox, a buzz
    of priests are nailing her in place,
    but moon repairs herself with cosmic glue

and floats to show her throat in Italy.
    There painted by Sandro Botticelli
    she rises lily thin in her white shoe.

In

Hawthorne's

Room

Of

Echoes

In Hawthorne's Room of Echoes, 1947

At Bowdoin College where H. Longfellow
and N. Hathorne were pals, Nathaniel changed
his name to Hawthorne to cut the shadow
and hang-rope of his Puritan deranged
great-great-grandfather Judge Hathorne who hung
the Salem heretics, or so he called
them. I live in Hawthorne's room, up a rung
of worn stairs, second floor, Longfellow Hall.
Ancestral fame was no help when young bards
Henry and Nathaniel were playing cards
for a jug of red wine, were caught, expelled,
and readmitted. At home they got hell.
In Hawthorne's room their snows sing in my veins;
their woods and haunted moon hum in my brain.

Moon, Keep Setting Back Clocks

Sometimes I feel, sometimes I don't, sometimes
I feel like a motherless child. When mom
was here I loved her, wanting out. No time
ever did I want her to leave. Please come
again tonight. I'll cook for you. We'll foxtrot
all over the house. Dad, you come too,
as Frost would say. Robert Frost, I miss you,
our lunch in Middletown. I'll set the clocks
so time will have a fit and let us be.
I'm cold tonight. Winter has sweatered me.
I'm hot as blazes through connections with
the catalog of blood and friends who make
me feel so full yet motherless. The shake
of snowy bells wakes me. I leave for myth.

Lune à Paris, 1948[4]

La lune d'hiver à Paris
dans son appartement de nuages
sort et danse folle parmi
peintres, savants, et le ménage
des jeunes poètes et rêveurs
qui partageant ses grands lacs blêmes
et blessants. Intime voleur
de cerveaux dans ma vie bohème,
j'aime surtout la demi-lune,
moitié habillée. Demi-garçon
ou taureau, je lis constamment
pour un rendez-vous, au moins une
fois, avec le gracieux oignon
du ciel dans ma soupe d'étudiant.

Moon in Paris, 1948

The winter moon in Paris
in her apartment of clouds
emerges and dances mad among
the painters, scholars, and the ménage
of young poets and dreamers
who share her great pale
yet wounding lakes. Intimate thief
of brains in my bohemian life,
above all I love the half-dressed
half-moon. Half a child
or bull, I read constantly
for a rendezvous, at least once,
with the beautiful onion
of the sky in my student soup.

Max Jacob the Day He Was Seized

by the Gestapo, February 24, 1944,
at the St. Benoît-sur-Loire Monastery

Picasso painted all night long. You slept
and when the Spaniard took the bed at dawn
in the small furnished room you shared, you leapt
back to the chair to scribble poems and yawn.
One bed and two young artists. You were poor
always. Then you saw light and moved your soul
in with the monks. You always played the fool
and wrote of butchers with binoculars,
dancing the streets of far Japan whose moon
had fleas. Your books shone in the libraries
of Paris—Max's caves. One afternoon
the Gestapo found you. Your monks tried to save
you. *J'ai ta peau!*⁵ you joked, mocking the lice
that bit you, bravely punning to the grave.

Isaak Babel the Day He Was Seized

by the NKVD, May 15, 1939, in Pereldelkino
and driven to the Lubyanka prison

Isaak could hardly ride his Cossack horse,
dashing through Poland with the young Red Guard
to free the peasants from their venal lords
and rape a Jew or two. In the back yard
he strangled a black goose on the Shabbat
and roasted it, and while the Hasids wept
their flaming tefillin and a tall black hat
sparked holy taste and helped him laugh. He slept
in drunken haylofts with his comrade sheep,
that merry man, Isaak, whose laugh was hot,
who wrote *Red Cavalry* but was a crypto czar,
they said, and should be tortured, tried and shot.
As the policemen threw him in the car
he turned to say, You guys don't get much sleep.

The Cow Jumps Over the Moon Where
Federico Ate Melons

The sun wears sheets of bestial light
hanging fresh in the woods, but where
is Lorca's moon? Must it be night
for moons to be? By day she's there,
a ghost of memory. In Spain
she glows for Federico. No,
she is his tombstone fire of pain
and passion. A cold moon rainbow
washes his dawn. The jumpy cow
sighs for him, wants moon plants to feast
on, leaps into felicity,
munches high sky grass, but no beast
can taste his old light. Who's left now
to help the murdered poet see?

The Death of the Wounded Child

by Antonio Machado, 1939

Again the hammer through the night is heard:
the fever in the bandaged temples of
the child. "Mother, look, the yellow bird!
and black and purple butterflies above!"
"Sleep now, my son." The mother near the bed
squeezes the little hand. "O flower of fire!
Who can squeeze you, tell me, O flower of blood?"
In the bleak room a smell of lavender.
Outside, the round moon is whitening dome
and tower across the city in its gloom.
Somewhere a droning plane one cannot see.
"Are you asleep? O flower of blood and gold."
The windows clamor on the balcony.
"O cold, cold, cold, cold, cold!"

Guillaume, a Berlin Diary, 1907

Café im Litteraturhaus, Berlin, 2010

Ich bin Guillaume Apollinaire
passant des beaux jours à Berlin
avec ein fräulein qui a l'air
of hating me. She does me in.
Moon-lost we stroll the Tiergarten.
She kisses me by a birch tree.
Hidden, she holds my dick. The sun
blesses our youth. Then she slaps me
and flees. I find her by the Rhine,
selling hot bread. You're a numbskull,
she says, but waves as my train whines
away. In Berlin I'm dark beer.
The years pass. I'm hit in the skull.
Her shells. My baker girl I fear.

Below the Tuberculosis Sanatorium Above Athens,

Men holding arms in bathrobes like to stroll
from marble Mount Penteli down the slope
to the olive tree zone near my house. All
have tuberculosis. Sometimes they smoke
Papastrátos 1. Quietly, in light
autumn clothes, they converse. I walk
with them. There is no cure yet but slow time
and sun and rest, and then good luck.
At the king's school I cross the German queen
about the rebels killed in camps. She frowns
but lends me books. Soon I'm expelled. "You're free,"
the men in pajamas say. I leave my town
for winter Mykonos. Moon beneath my sneakers,
with my sick friends we stroll the lone sea.

A Kid Making It with the Hudson Moon Who Is a Savvy Dame, 1939

When I run home into the polar wind
booming along the street, the moon is calm
and almost still, a yellow peach who sinned
naked and lusciously over the lamb
of gully snow. She stands perfect above
the Hudson River, her vagina warm
as the fat taxis where the dopes in love
make out, speeding along the Drive. No harm,
I think, and Eliot can prove those oddballs
grab each other's tits and prick. No one
can look inside, except the wind that blew
near by. I heave onto my bed, my rod
is steel, my eyes a mess of fire and fun.
That sky lady in the sky I kiss her blue.

Fading Back to Our Polish Shtetl and Black Hats

The spring is late this year. Its winds are raw,
aching a bit. The moon is full. I pad
down through the gully to Salt Creek. The law
of seasons will prevail, ending the sadness
of dead grass, and soon my winter in
the barn will end. I fade lonely in space
back to my roots next door to a Ukraine
of vast jade fields and to that other race
inside their ghetto villages. Black hats
and books in velvet. My ancestors? Gone
a century, that blood was me. I pass
today. Since grass can't know it is the grass,
I spot no wings of mystic chariots,
yet in my blood the moon burns on and on.

Moon Bird

The Persians say she is the nightingale
of memory. Although she's never heard,
her song persists through windows of a jail
or childhood eyes. Unlike the poet's bird
she's visible most every night, and when
a cloud or sunshade blocks her out, we see
her memory in Leopardi. In his pen
both are the burning virgin. Ecstasy
of standing elsewhere is their common plight,
that beautiful escape from solitude.
Shining without oxygen, a stone mirror
her brain, the moon bird knows each single night
of history. Alexander in the nude
draws maps below her breasts and dreams of terror.

Constant Moon, I Long for You

If you, moon, were half as loony as me,
you'd fall out of your orbit into
vague eternity,
and vagabond forever to the inn
of two heartbeats that you can never reach.
Then you would hike the curving grass
of space, roll down the beach
of platitudes inhabiting the glass
vacuum that experts on the earth detect
though Galileo's telescope,
and join me as a friend
of maps. But you are constant and elect
our naked separation. Hope
burns nightly though I dread my lunar end.

Moon God of Silence

Moon god, you're cooler than our God
whom Gnostics angrily decry
for bashing body love and troding
on good Eve. Today we sigh
or pray or beg and yet God won't
reveal himself, and you are here
immense and beautiful. You don't
deceive us through grim priests of fear
who hawk tortures of Hell. And still
you let us down. I am at fault
and want too much. You glare. I see
your endlessly romantic hills
yet think of Lot's pillar of salt.
Your silence leaves me only me.

Naked Sea of Serenity

You do so much for me I shouldn't crab
about your bare Mare Tranquilita-
tis (Sea of Serenity), dumb mouth. I blab
to you as to my dog, Bucky. *Bah, bah,*
he growls discreetly, and at least he turns
in recognition. You turn too. And O
good friend, we've spent so many nights stern
in austere Spain or circles on the snow
of pine tree Maine. Picasso hears me moan
about my blues and draws us with his heart
of turpentine to quash my plaint. What luck!
Eternal pal, I'll go on whispering groan
and worry, lust, and fear about this art
of death, and we'll do everything but fuck.

Moon Faces in a Misty Sock

My life is up and down. I bitch, you roar
at me, winking behind a misty
sock. You spend your bookish life, a bore
of repetitions in the fist
of measurable rotations, though your face
has names like Mare Nectaris—
Sea of Nectar—or, closer to my case,
Mare Crisium—Sea of Crisis.
And I would like to throw the towel in,
jump off a cliff or at least hang
out safe, though under house arrest, and pin
my face to yours for sleep and dream.
You can't care less whether I live or bang
my brains out while you grin and beam.

Dylan Looks Great, 1953

Dylan looks younger than his beer-fat years,
the master of delight. Sitting just rows
from *Under Milkwood,* I hear every sphere
of Welsh babble roll from the bawdy glow
and echo of his lips. These are his last
utterances to a crowd. I leave the room
for glassy mist on 92nd, pass
from Y to Central Park night freeze. Moon gloom
breaks through high wool. In the Village downtown
Dylan picks up his jigger till the roaring
lad fans out. Saint Vincent's.[6] No one's guessed
Thomas was to write a grand opera for
Stravinsky. Dylan is a diabetic.
Docs give him wrong pills. The opera drowns.

I Spinoza,

Lens Grinder

in the

Amsterdam Ghetto,

Make the Moon

Live

I Spinoza, Lens Grinder in the Amsterdam Ghetto, Make the Moon Live

Since sky is our spiritual space, I wish
to merge in space and keep the moon alive.
She's everywhere and God's left hand. A fish
and planet fill my lens. Though them I dive
into the heart where I can study soul
whose light is numbered rain. Caligula
ordered his slaves to catch the moon and roll
her to his throne. I own that cupola
laughing in heaven and I'm not a nut
or wise man. I just look and she is mine.
My ghetto moon teams with the Sephardim
evoking our old Spain. She feeds me dream
to shape the cosmos. With my pen I cut
the sky through Latin glass for soul to shine.

Scrawling in Cafés, I Dream Up a Moon Feast in Her Delicious Kitchen

A lousy cook, I burn water or forget the eggs
till they explode and hit the ceiling like
buckshot. So I haunt cafés. My legs
are European and take me on my bike
to every table in the city. There,
tired of caffeine but glad to read or write
in solitude, I spend my years. I fear
a guilty past, worry about the sight
of faces I must face; my skinny being
can't sleep. Yet when I'm eating a swordfish
and scrawling, then I'm moon glad. Overhead
the moon has her delicious kitchen. Seeing
her—even in my mind—I dream her dish,
her face of yogurt, honey, cheese and bread.

Dark Side of the Moon

A third of life is sleep. I sleep with her
whenever I can focus dream and lust.
So sperm and moon make my thermometer
of joy. I'm high. But when I walk the crust
of this blue planet, I look down and drag
my neck and sorrows with my maudlin heart.
I'm not too proud. I'd rather dance, yet sag,
and even if I had the will, I'm smart
enough not to glance at the truth of sun.
But if the galley slaves in Plato's cave
escape in John's dark night and not high noon,
they will be cool, not blind, and light not stun
them into mystic knowing. So I save
my eyes and neck through night and walk the moon.

Moon Shower in Her Tub of Earth

I like to shower with the moon and do
it early while she's bright and full. I glide
into her tub. She's glistening; and true
to form she takes me to her hidden side.
We close our eyes. The water fills her cracks
and hills and in the shadows we embrace.
Rolling together, Moon and Earth, our backs
the surface of a deep celestial space
of private rendezvous, we press and cling
tighter not to fall off and disappear.
We dance. The moon is candidly in love
with me. I soap her crevices and sing,
and she, squeezing me to her atmosphere,
beams me, drops me, crushes me from above.

Full Moon Over a Two-Note Man in Windy South Dakota

Full moon, I am a two-note man. I toot
on high or low. Tonight I'm low in bed,
and low despite the wonder of you, brute
glow ball bounding through the window. Sour lead
winter moon face, last night you stood over
my car racing beyond the exit on
the South Dakota interstate. Earlier,
I walked shivering through night-bleak Vermillion
under your hardware smile. Soon mud, then spring.
I am a funeral bell, low high, a bag
of coffins prancing under your dark lips.
I can't drag up to drink or write. The sting
of mercy pounds in me until I sag
absorbed into your mouth and blazing hips.

Lunar Salvation

What kind of man am I to fall in love
with a shepherd hound and the moon? A dog
and rock. The hound is gone. The mystique of
a life, a breath when it is squelched, may jog
the memory, but the gross reality
of presence has the bite. Absence is cruel
against the dead—and us their lovers. We
survive. That's all. The moon is neither fool
nor god. It is a circulating rock,
a child of natural law like us. I need
her. She enthralls me fully and I stick
with her till I am moon dust, with my flock
of soulless song confessions few will read.
I give her life and am her lunatic.

Comrade Moon

Comrade moon, you and I go deep. It rains.
Thunder clouds cup the earth, hiding your sphere
of sympathy, but you're not locked in chains
and rotate seen or not. You're there to cheer
me with your being. I give you names and know
I've made a rock my bible, and I swear
by it, by the illusion of the O
of light, the evening friend swallowing air
like me. There is a risk and sadness. I
need you and love you till the night I drop
to moonlessness. I do my best to hold
your glow inside. You light me, and your eye
thrills, a benign LSD, a wild shop
of life. I stare at you until I'm cold.

New Moon in la Douce France

Luxembourg Gardens. Afternoon.
I daydream (Machado's habit)
I may not die tonight. The moon
lying on her back in orbit,
a gold romantic, slips. This shrimp
knows she is thin and how she looks.
I wave *so long,* swallow a mint,
improve my breath. While my ass cooks
I beat the rap and wake. This tale
puzzles me. How jaunty! My scheme
is hop out of my funeral dance:
starve death to death, make the moon scream.
On this spring afternoon in France
the new moon waves its skinny veil.

Old Orchard Plane and a Sad Black Moon, 1933[7]

When I flew at Old Orchard Beach with dad,
I was just five. He squeezed me by his side
in a two-wing open cockpit plane. We had
habits of the future moonwalkers, pride
in modern motors, watches of the air
to cart us spinning in the sun. We spun
a spider's nest to catch our fall, to spare
the earth of nutrient blood. But one Sun-
day in bright May, with no chute or balloon
or winged silver clock of heaven, he,
like me in Orange, Mass., leaps through the brute
air of Saint John. I wear a parachute
and pull the cord, but dad is pure. The sea
of death calms care. He drops, a sad black moon.

After Calamity, Eat Tapioca

After calamity only green stars
and Mexican moustache that children hang
their toys from. Small red planes circle my car
yet how far are the scorpions who sang?
I watch the shadows of three suicides
and chase a would-be kill across the night-
sea till the victim wakes with miles to ride
before her gloom sky breaks to heron white
of snowy Africa. Unlock the moon,
undo her coarse gray blouse. Unlock the sea
so fish and submarines will float below
the mind again and kill calamity.
Darkness far. Peaceable I row and row.
The hangman's out to lunch. Don't come back soon.

Prairie Rose Moon

The prairie rose moon blowing on the glass
of heaven hangs a moment on a bud
of fire. A windy angel, I am pass-
ing through. Her dignity, like Billy Budd
swinging forever from the mast, compels
her permanence of rolling flame. I stare.
Her colors signify what Shakespeare tells
photographers: "Click, but you cannot bare
my real identity. Stick to my light
and leave my blood and face alone." I guess
I'm like the rest. I want to know. Perhaps
because I don't know me inside, a mess
of words ticking to dead-end night. By night
I see her rose with hope and then collapse.

The New Moon Rose

The new moon rose, the old moon in her arms.
I am an old moon jogging in the night,
blissfully panting out to strawberry farms.
Jogging isn't a sin. Age is the blight
of nature, yet I'll smooch and dream, a dog
in paradise, pissing on clouds until
I croak. I push the body as I jog,
hoping it won't break up. I'd rather spill,
downed by a busted heart than a soft chair.
No choice. I'm terrified by mind, not death,
as I spot dark inside. Stars came out soon
after a week of rain and gray nightmare
of months. Now racing night thrills me with breath.
When gone I'll spin my laps on a black moon.

Letter to the Moon

I write a letter to the sun
and ask to let it rain for one
more year. And then I write the moon
and ask to let me see her noon
of midnight in a storm of light.
Then star and satellite hit back
with bureaucratic silence black
and total. Then I use Kabal-
lah numbers to get through. No mail
comes out. I hire a nightingale
to sing. I think they'll love it, but
when I lie down and beg, they cut
me off. So I give up. I die
a while. It works. They rain and sigh.

Moon Lady at the Bar

I take her to a bar. That's not my shtick
but she can glow like no one else, and she's
a sport. I'm feeling empty, vague, and sick
with boredom. If I read a book, I'd squeeze
it for a gripping plot or one bright thought.
My moon lady has class. I like her can-
did beams. She's like a female astronaut
and we're together in a soaring phan-
tom rocket. Don't belittle her, that great
contagious woman. As I look around
I'm chatting with myself. The moon's outside,
watching me mope and drink my lonely state
of nothing into the despairing ground
and if I claim she dates me, I have lied.

Moon Sleep

Year after year I've wanted her and come
to empty fields with cloudless firmaments
and with my naked eye I soon become
a lunatic abandoning all sense
of time. The moon is infinitely near,
a step away. I touch her toes, her soft
and empty mountains. In her Buddha ear
her gold ravines are literate. I cough
up courage and plunge in. She wel-
comes me. Her dazzling grace lightens my head.
As I worm into her complacent face,
she feels like heaven or an icy hell.
Vanishing into her orgasmic space,
I sleep on her in light time of the dead.

Moon Trees, Moon Beasts

Moon trees, moon beasts. Hounds race the plains, and rats,
gray baby rats, wake under subway walls,
yelping for tits and warmth. The evening bats
are busy testing radar. They were balls
of sleeping rodents waiting to explode
and skit through night. I gave moon watches to
my children who are wandering the globe,
looking, like me, for Euclid with his clue
for making lines eternal. Moon trees, lun-
ar dreams. Huge insect Selenites are glad,
logical and concealed inside the moon.
Moon teeth, moon eyes inhabit glassy light
in my bad sleep. The oceans have gone mad
and rise and bellow storms in lunar white.

Humpty Dumpty Falls Off the Moon

I'm writing sonnets to the moon, yet all
is Humpty Dumpty tumbling down. Okay.
I'm fine, although the college library calls
to say you're out. You can't take books today
or ever. Health insurance cut. Out of
control. Life sucks. I can't get it together,
papers a mountain, sleep a pit. But love
is everywhere, so why complain? My mother
told me, "Scrub the sink, mister," when I washed
the dishes. Why didn't that metaphor
sink in? I'm writing sonnets to the moon
who helps me get up from the dismal floor
of going broke. I'm crazy as a loon
and lunar blasted. In the dark I'm squashed.

Moon Escape

I love the moon and so am slapped in jail,
escape, hunted, and, when the bloodhounds
pick up the scent, I'm caught, held without bail
until a trial for lunacy has found
me guilty of moon love and negligence
of normalcy. I loved the new moon once
in Egypt. I am meeting common-sense
Ibrahim, my grave-robber friend who hunts
antiquity, a patriarch and seer
of marketable beauty, who sells the eye
of the small sphinx. We meet and share a beer.
I buy the moon. Cheap. His two wives are pissed.
Enraged he shoots his pistol at the sky,
but I escape, the moon safe in my fist.

Moon Sitting on a Twilight Rainbow

I feel a touch of entropy. My watch
ticks forward while my memory tick-flicks back
to scenes that hassle me. Clock time will botch
body and brain, but I'm on guard to sack
the rodent. Good food, workout. When I see
the wolf moon sitting on a twilight rain-
bow, I pause elsewhere, beyond physics. Theory
can wait chatting with science. See the plane
of flashing wolf moon rainbow, a brain chip
opening at midnight. Can the failed hand
of an old poet tap his keys and send
eternity across a page? As I mend
my lungs with pills, ecstasy is land
mortgaged, the port before the last black ship.

Patient Moon

The moon is not impatient like the son
of man who cleans the lepers, and the eye
around the planet washing her green sun
of midnight on a few whose meadows cry
for sperm, maddens the people of the boats
with milk flaming on rock. Yet even when
she floods a dying child, she never floats
out of her craters with the oxygen
of faith, nor lords us with a vision ray
of crystal heaven. Full and filled with sand,
her face is the death object in the night,
is now and nebulous. While mystery and
the black moon in my head eclipse all light,
she wakes Edison to fix my blurry clay.

The Rolling Cosmos

Cosmos is deaf. My heart is bumping fear. Go!
Roll on, dumb globe. I light a gas lamp to keep
her real and on her roll. Nothing can slow
or speed the globe in her infinite leap
outward into the lonely Christmas lights
of stars and moons and roaring cosmic scrap.
I chew a bit of moon on squirmy nights.
My dream valves stir cool Edens while I nap.
Our globe rolls on as long as I keep
her wolfing quiche. No blue-haired cop can blow
a whistle and slow down our big bang blast
into dark energy. My nightmares grow.
I check my stopwatch breath on earth. I last.
Our globe rolls on while I gulp air below.

Spooking the Sea of the Firmament

The universe is such a waste. I read
its beauty in dominions of far sparks
that are more dream than suns. On our blue bead
of earth I push my breath, jogging on parks
until one year I'll join the waste of flesh
beneath the earth while those brown dwarfs and moons
and bigger stars are dumb without a fresh
cucumber or a woman's tongue. Some tunes
of Mozart's piano ping across the brow
of Mercury. It's all a spaceship can
cook up to gentrify infinities
of sand. Armed with hooks, bait by the ship bow,
I float out into void, a fisherman
guessing what soul I'll drag up from dead seas.

Du Fu Recalling Li Bai and His Moon Swan

December night almost freezes us, but
a bowl of wine, the dishes on the floor
in Ming-bright China, keeps our smelly cot-
tage hot with fun. These days when we are poor,
neither of us holds a post. We both failed
the imperial texts. Imagine asking us
how to compose a poem! Your daughter sailed
to Peach Blossom Spring. The black octopus
of hunger strangled her. My head is white
in mourning for my youth. Good Li, you drink
a lot and write a lot. The moon looks on.
We walk outside. I'm turning blue. You fight
the horror of our villages of ink
on fire, while overhead you spot your swan.

Heavenly Pals

The moon I always want to hump and love
and treat as the austere beauty of the night.
She is the other sex, a Spanish dove,
a falcon climbing blind and cloaked in light,
a dazzling lady with no place to rest.
You sun, another jock, a man I walk
with every day, you are a poacher, beast,
a tramp. You search and scavenge like a hawk
while filling me with breath and dance and go.
God with his many faces can't be seen.
Not in his books. So God invisible
is less real than your boiling bath. I know
at least you are. We always schmooze. I'm Bill,
you are moon, sun, my soul—my lie—and clean.

Below the Quarter Moon

Don't be a Buddhist skinhead gal
gazing through clouds of emptiness
around a Bhutan peak of eternal
absence! This unholy mess
on the sidewalk spots your peekaboo
face dropping pails of dream
or nasty nightmare I wake to.
Moon dancer, you obey laws, yet scheme
to be the ultimate slow full-moon mime
artist, walking-in-place Jean Louis Barrault
costumed in glaring chalk.
Forget your running shoe. You will grow
and glow but I shall box the pox of time
so we can pause and talk.

Gospel of Light

The moon is natural in the evening. I
cannot be angry at it. And a flute
high on the mountain is the sweetest lie
of separation. And the stench of fruit,
fogging the blasted lots, over the quake
in the Algerian city, joins the dead
who don't smell sweet. Yet in the inner lake
of light, *lake of the heart* as Dante said,
the rays are stronger than the suffering
and rapture of the outer world. To be
inside and be the light is everything
I want. Yet now I live seized by the wall,
those ten walls of the flesh in which I see
pure ignorance, that is, nothing at all.

Black Moon on Way to Vets

I am blind laughing, the world's a radio,
I hear an Oakland gunshot near the Vets
(I'm one), tune in a gang of friends below
my brain. Winter morning. I drive poorly
and spot nothing inside this wind-up doll
created to spit out her grammar tree
of words at you. Now with my milky dead
eyes, I lurch by the Technical High School,
a wheelchair pushed by a guy with a beard
coffin long, screaming: *Never been so happy!*
Then a blind woman with a black moon
locked in her handbag comes up beside me.
Together we consume her moon-rich bread.

Sunday Morning in Fascist Spain, 1951

We motorbike through Spain of Isabel
la Católica and Franco *el toro
de la muerte* and iron hand. The belle
of our farm house, the eyes of tomorrow,
is Soledad, who is ten, blond, sigh-eyed,
lovely. Her dad killed a *guardia civil,*
a tricorne hat with leather soul. He fled
and she's an orphan. She lives on the hill
where the Carthaginian cemetery
cabins the poorest of our village. She
hangs out with us. Justo the Gypsy sledge-
hammers the highway black and strums
his sea-guitar carnation white. Our ledge
is Roman pink rhapsodic by March plums.
Andalusia! Most of her grand poets die,
flee, yet Lorca's moons glare in a child's eye.

SUNBOOK

Dancing

Greek

with Kerouac

Until

Dawn's

Sun

Dancing Greek with Kerouac Until Dawn's Sun

His first version of *On the Road* Jack wrote
in French, *Sur le Chemin*, taking his queue
from Dante's "Midway on the road."[8] His boat
of fame sails him to work and drink, a brew
that bombs. He dies at forty-seven. Years
I pal with Jack are wild. Greg brings Jack up
from New York with the gang. After ten beers,
Corso claims he's the only straight who's slept on top
of Jack o-Lantern. "Allen's a whore. All
are whores." Sobering up, Jack says, "I climbed the peak,
climbed Mount Tamalpais at dawn, and on
the summit saw Satori!" "You saw bull-
shit." "I saw bullshit," Jack says. His wife's Greek.
"Let's dance." And we dance Greek until Zen dawn.

Hassapiko: Greek Butcher's Dance

*Inspired by Manos Hadzidakis's music
and Nikos Gatsos's lyrics*

O my sun, O my sun,
O my king, don't leave me today.
   Now clouds, now clouds, have won
   my heart. Bleeding boy,
villains seized you, took you away.

   The Romans moved at dawn,
bound you, speared you, they crucified
   you in the afternoon.
   To everyone they lied—
forsaken one—and then you died.

   Tell me why, O my sun,
they envied you, were so upset.
   You lit my world with fun,
   you blazed, you were my bet.
I walked with you and then you set.

Sun

Sun is the eye up there. A glaring, black,
impossible-to-look-at fire. It creeps
on insects, under water, in the crack
of falcon cliffs, on fuzzy eggs. It sleeps
on beads of planets strung on cosmic rings.
Its hydrogen explosions warm the flute
of rays poking through moon clouds, and its wings
of morning celebrate the garden fruit
with hymns of life. On gum and cinnamon
and every spice it heats the chlorophyll.
When Galileo looked through flaming glass
for truth, he almost burned. Its miracle
alone makes light, the eye inside, a gas
of yellow worlds and black night without sun.

The Sun Can't Know He Is the Sun

The sun can't know he is the sun, nor light
know she is light. I fall in love
when I am born because I breathe the night
of life, a darkness fading as the dove
of flame feeds me on milk. My mother sighs
and takes me home. Sun gives me air
and time. In such good space I never die
and get to know I am. And I am rare,
the only body holding me. The sun
gives everything: a bed, a book
of spices. When Columbus finds this land,
the Mayas wear the sun but have no gun
against the cross. Sun in my hand
gives free light till he zaps me like a crook.

A Sunny Room at Mount Sinai, 1955

Mount Sinai Hospital. My mother lay
in a good corner room with lots of sun.
The surgeon traced the steps of her death dance.
A soldier then, I'd flown in from France
where in Périgueux's children's ward, one day
I saw a young girl in a coma. Sun
came through glass walls; the child was beautiful,
her face freshened with youth. Only inside
the cancer stormed. I saw the nun place wool
soaked in cold alcohol on her. She died
that afternoon. My mother's gown was loose
and she told us the awful things they'd done
when testing her downstairs. I see her eyes
today. She too was fresh and live. Some juice
lay undrunk by her pillow. A surprise
of pain. I left the room and she was gone.

In Sun and Soon in Coffins, 1955

A child's death cannot be explained.
I wonder why the lovely French
girls I see in a Catholic hospital
in lush Dordogne countryside
will soon die at nine or ten.
They lie unconscious on their beds,
their faces gazing at the ceiling.
These young faces appear healthy.
Cancer rages inside them. They
are not in pain, they are still. In
white gowns they linger in the sun
passing through glass walls they can't see.
In stunning beauty and peace they
will cease breathing and go where no
child should go. Nature has no heart.

A Pine Tree Talks to Me Under Green Maine

Why did those pancreatic cells gone bad
parade as half your life? It seized the floor
your early death, as you became a nomad
in the last weeks. You laughed as you left shore
on the Greek liner floating you to Greece.
Then dehydration on the ship, X-rays
in Athens that revealed the hopelessness,
Paris where I met your tears, a few days
in New York. And you sank from sun. Our blind
authorities of soul copped out—the Lord
and Lady up in heaven sipped their tea.
I came from you. You lived alone and signed
out dignified and patient on the board
that coffined you to Maine to feed a tree.

Mother

While you are lowered in the clay
we weep under the summer sun.
The rocking of the coffin done,
our meager party goes away.
You leave so quickly for the night
almost no one on the great earth
observes the moment of your death.
We few who knew your quiet light
try to remember, yet forget,
and neither memory nor talk
will bring you sun once it has set.
Your life was brief—a morning walk.
We whom you loved still feel an O
of horrid absence in Maine snow.

Father Imitating Angels Amid the Colorado Rockies

I wonder what my father thought
climbing the stairway to the door
that opened on the roof. "I ought
to turn around and calm the roar
of failures and begin again.
It's May in Colorado and
with Van Gogh on my wall I can
make it." He finds the knob, his hand
wavers. No, he was very drunk
with pain, his eyes were gone, he had
the smile of the detached. In May
we all got lost and he had sunk
to punishment. In sun my dad
ghosted to the edge and flew away.

London Morning

Someone loves me and I love her.
Let every bell in London toll
loud the news. Grief cannot prosper
while we sleep arm in arm and bowl
the moon-sick morning sun across
her mother city, lighting rags
and riches with her rays that toss
us out of bed, that boss the stags
and jaguars on the pampas, clean
eyelids of ocean bubbles in-
to union with huge hugging waves.
Love waits darkly while postmen lean
against the snow to bring the sin
of joy and wake the blind. Sun saves.

Good Morning, Busie Old Fool, Unruly Sun

Good morning, starship, morning sun.
NASA won't fund you but you're not
melancholy or sick. John Donne
adores you when he's a young hot
cocksman. You lie upon sheets. He
and his hot Anne giggle to see light
ramble across the Thames and ski
around the globe. They sit upright,
then screw, make kids to hide their dust,
are sailors painting death's dry lip
with your bright kiss. When Jack gets old
and pious, God blinks and changes lust
to night; Donne dies robed in black gold
to catch a star and circle round the sun.

No Smoke, but Sun in Lungs

Even in London and dark poison smog,
between drizzles I like to walk in sun
and count my friends and with the poets jog
along the Thames to catch the Cockney puns
or Macbeth's howl far as the Isle of Skye
and Inner Hebrides. The sun goes where
there's life, even sunk in the soggy sky
of human lungs. Today, as if *All Clear!*
had just rung out, the nurse says you will live
tomorrow, so forget the hearse, you're clean,
the X-ray of your right lung negative
except for scarring. Goodbye to old Dance
of Death who beckons kings and cocks, the mean
and kind, to wear the same headdress of trance
and shade. Blake comes for tea with his sun key,
opens all coffins & sets us children free.

Black Sun of Felicity

There is a heart of darkness. She is sweet,
is terror, is cyclamen white. Look long
as you drop down and see her words—not street-
chat drivel—and the darkness makes her tongue
Scarlatti clear. Meadow lamb, turtledove
of canticles, hyena jaws reside
at the black seafloor in our heart where love
is not until you glare it live. Abide
with a ruby love born in Burma. Make
her sensual sheets flap in the secret sun
of choral sky, rainbow brain, in the lake
of Dante. Traherne's cows float at black noon
of night to leap over the happy moon.
Black sun glows in the heart. Our fires are one.

Sun Rises and Ceases to Shine

The sun rises and then ceases to shine.
Kohelet[9] claims he communes with his heart,
looking for wisdom. I commune with mine,
looking through layers and layers of the dark.
The golden bowl is broken, books undone,
yet sweet is light and eyes gazing at sun.
There is a time to live, a time to die.
Earth gives and takes. Vainly I am alone;
after I'm taken I won't even sigh
and so I joy. Some look at me as stone.
I am not mad. They look at me with scorn
because I grow less in their eyes—old Joe
Blow Hard. We are poor sad shits; we are born
to chance the days. I pen what I don't know.
It comforts me to be in ignorance.
In this lone hall I hope my shoes will dance.

Sun Is Our Star

Sun is our maker star, the moon our child;
earth a hunk of sun, moon a bite of earth.
Earth strolls around the sun and prints the birth
of time upon his cosmic clock. No wild
behavior in their astral shop. The sun,
a bright professor of astronomy,
has tenure. No firing him. By now he's done
hurling out planets. An infinity
of stars jealously sparkles over our ball
of oceans, wars and drones, and they dully wait
forever lifeless, banging upon ships
to nowhere while our sun and moon—a double doll
floating on fire and frozen lakes—skate
and when they cross they tango their eclipse.

Sun Is Laughter of the Cosmos

The sun is gas on fire and so he lights
and livens, kills. The moon is rock but sends
no death rays to the tanner. The sun bites
the skin with fatal pleasures that he lends
for free. I love him like a father. He
is laughter of the cosmos, the close friend
amid the stars blinding with rhapsody
when we feel one. Like God, sun has no end
of names although we cannot look him in
the face. In all the countries I love most
he's joy. In France he marries me. A pin
of death starts to scratch blots on my skin—
for now I've blocked him. Sun, heavenly host,
your lethal beauty might make me a ghost.

In Burma Monks Wear Sun Cloth on Their Loins

The sun is wonderful. He likes to come
and light the gloom away. His voice at dawn
is birdful. Once in Burma, drinking rum
all night with our jeep driver, bouncing on
back roads, sun wakes us with a glitter and
a cloud wink. Asia is an ancient piece
of planet, wearing paddies on the land
and inner sun to capture inner peace.
The monks wear sun cloth on their loins. At four,
hungry, wiped out from the road, we stop
to eat at a truck stop. They throw wet dough
against the oven wall, and bread cakes pour
like moonlight on our plates. We bribe the cops
to push on north. The free sun lets us go.

Pushcart Sun in the Gobi Desert

The father sun is friendly with each son,
with Chinese deserts. He camps out on them,
filling the Gobi with oblivion
and yurts, Gnostics, the white freshwater gem
of pearls that fill the pushcarts in the markets.
On the planet's lowest plain I run
all morning through the oxygen-rich air,
take breathers in cold streams. Here in Xinjang,
old Turkestan, the sun and I are pals.
Under his gaze I wrestle with a Turk,
share soup, walk to an abandoned white mosque,
dome eye of mystery by the night canals
of tyranny as in Tibet. The clerk
of heaven, punctual star, laughs in his kiosk.

Sunjoy by the Blue Monastery on the White Cycladic Island

I like to slap my body on the sand
and fry exultantly as much as I
can bear. Eyes closed I feel a laughing hand
on me. Gold beach. Greek island. Solstice sky.
I love to stroll the surf edge to the near
blue monastery, *Agios Sostis,* sit
on huge boulders, stare out at *Voos,* the Steer,
lonely rock beast bright on the sea. I eat
tomatoes, bread and grapes. No pain today.
One year I live in a stone house made of
fat cubes of sun. Iceberg isle. The architect
is whitewash. Jasmines raise the night. Sunday
brings watermelon pyramids. Above
the quay, gulls, briny wind. Sun is perfect.

The Lilies

The lilies in the field below a sphere
of half moons in the rain, of fowls and moths,
go unclothed, do not spin or toil or hear
the prayer of Solomon in radiant cloths,
and yet their nakedness is perfect snow
under whose textiled galaxies the seed
lies comatose. The lilies only grow
and burn. Their meditation is to feed
on light. Naked of thought, a multitude
by the day Adam learned to stand, these plants
are human, living in chance villages
like breezy monks sworn to mute elegance.
When thrown into the oven, no lord says
a word. The lilies fall in solitude.

Lapland

The roots of the earth protrude
down into the pinegray ocean
and up into the glacial snow.

There are not many fir trees
as we push into the unreal
north. We are beyond the green

and on nude scrubby earth again.
Here where snow yawns into the
sea, and air is clean like fish,

distance and form and seasons
are more true than the odd boat
or village. Time. This land is

dream—planet where almost no one
is—or if real, then quick cities
south are dream before the slow

iceland. At night sunshine floats
on big mountain ribs of snow;
gulls cry and cod run in the ocean.

Starting in Paris, 1948

It is a beautiful day. The sun blows shiny
on the magnolia. The rhododendron
near Annapurna glows with laughter, tiny
rose eyes below the mountain snow horizon
as we trek at breathless heights. At the lodge,
freezing, we eat scraps in stinging smoke-
air by the fire. I think back to my dodge
with crime in Paris. First night, a bad joke
when the maid nabs my trousers from my grip.
Down at the zinc bar, in my French beret,
I take two hardboiled eggs, order cognac
and black coffee. Rapture! There on my back
at l'Hôtel Vert I can't guess I will trip
around the globe my typhoid-Mary way.

Bestiary Lion

The lion sleeps with one eye open to the dawn.
His third eye dreams HE is the militant of God,
who after disappearing for three days will yawn
back into life and save us from the mortal sod.
Yet normally the monarch lion wakes by sun
and with a mortal bite he chokes a zebra for
his pride of golden ladies and his cubs, and one
day when the sun strolls on a cloud, with a mad roar
he leaps into the sky, and with a mammoth bite
swallows the sunstar, blackening the globe in night.
Now, lions are the handsomest of quadrupeds,
but watch out for these feline charmers in their pride,
who with a scream will turn a world to dread.
Tame killers, if you can, or keep them on your side.

Peacock

The peacock is the Sun King of the birds,
Louis Quatorze, but in captivity,
with no poor workers leaping to his words.
His feathered splendor glows for fans to see.
He is the pet of beauty on a farm,
not in the bush for hunters or wild teeth.
His arrogance is slow and does no harm
to subjects since he has none. He's a wreath
of poetry to amuse a wishful Yeats
deep in the Congo, formed by nature's eye
green like his train, but when he lifts his tail
to mate he grows enormous like a whale.
This pheasant, no way peasant, struts and eats
until his owner pines for peacock pie.

Old Elephant in Her Bath

Below Kilimanjaro in these wetlands
is paradise for wading in the mud
and water. Mammoths stand on massive hands,
their pillar legs glimmer in stinking crud.
In a small pond an elder elephant
cools off and joys. Far off the green hills chant,
the local wind has settled on his black
back wrinkling the sun. But when this sack
of nature's hugest beast begins to sink,
he struggles in the slippery swamp. In a wink
his ears float like wings. Only a haunched leg
and tusks are visible. Then as if beg-
ging light, his tusks shudder a second, fade,
and so the older elephant is shade.

Big Shot Sun, Ultimate Wise Guy

You got a lot going for you, big shot.
You're the gang boss, what you say goes, or oops,
you lay your watch down on the sky and blot
the light, clotting my eyes, and your night troops
assemble, dump me off a dock into
the Hudson. Nothing to it. So I play
along. Plato has your number, sees through
your blinding gaze, makes you a mystic ray
Plotinos grabs to free the soul and make
you One with it. The seer is the seen.
Like a hit man savior you'd turn me into
toast to merge with you. Give me a break.
I need more time and space. Though I have been
a loner, and sun is friendly, I'll burn clean.

God or a Tunic of Light

There is no God, but a tunic of light
wakes the twilight tasting of cellos blue
like the eyeball of sky starting to brighten
teeth and Chinese factories that spew
coal ants through children's lungs. The healing sun
on Greek white island olives keeps no blog
on other presences and powers. I run
from God, yet keep more mystery than a bog
of Irish nightingales and Celtic hair.
Intact and now, I love imperfect mind,
moons of inlight. I am complexity
like you. A black tunic of night bugs me.
Biology will tick my heart to blind
nothing yet I am now. Poor would-be ghost,
God can't catch cold. Lungless he'd love sweet air
like humanoids. I leave him my French toast.

In Cambridge Upset with Sun Because We Disappear

The pearly sun and alabaster moon
come faithfully to Cambridge through the mist
and rains. Their earthly faces glow or swoon
in cloud cloth but they always show. I miss
my son and friends who walked these crooked brick
sidewalks. Borges sees Emerson among
these shadows. Blind, he always sees. The trick
of memory and conjecturing has hung
all tenses in the mind. Sun sets the pace
for time yet mindlessly ignores that soon
we skip and others come. He doesn't care.
The sun is impish bright, his morning face
on beds of lovers, striping naked hair
with heat. I brood, complaining to the moon.

Sir Sun and Lady Moon

Sir Sun and Lady Moon, a paradigm
of goodness, perfect man and wife,
both Platonists, once they were one round rhyme
in space. Each longs for eyes, for life
of snowy peace. Their mission is to warm,
charm, create love not jealousy.
Silently active, they will never harm
for pleasure. Self-reliant, free
of greed and hate, they model beauty, give
eternity and pensive soul
to me—the sweet illusion. Though I sigh,
Sir Sun and Lady Moon forgive
my torment that one awful night I die.
Through night and day they light me whole.

Pamplona Café in the Sun

In an outdoor café off Harvard Square,
I'm sitting in the sun, reading the work
of a black waiter who's asking me where
to sell it. Good luck. I too have had to lurk
outside the store, waiting. My soles are thin,
my hair not bad, yet life is time. The sun
would let me come, but it is boiling in
his photosphere. Back on the square a nun
toots her harmonica, a thin guy sits
against the wall, relaxed. HOMELESS WITH AIDS
his sign reports. He's beautiful. His wits
are sharp, I'm sure. It's time for God, it's time
for God to show. Please show. We all are made
of flesh, yet God or sun can't spare a dime.

Napping by the Charles River in Hot Sun

In Boston gentle sun glows on the phlox
and zinnias in this public park. The Jap-
anese are snapping pictures of me, the fox
among the Latin sheep. I like to nap
along the rows of flowers sucking the sky.
I'm so excited I must play the blind
man, close my eyes, and be the summer fly
a hand will sweep away. The sun is kind
to madmen and the poor: a democrat,
Walt Whitman among pigeons or San-
cho Panza joking on La Mancha plains.
My sun is blind to ethnic habitat,
and while I breathe he greets me as a swan
of hope. And when I'm dead he'll cool my pains.

Sun on Moon

The sun even touches against the ice
of Jupiter's Europa, one of her
sixteen true moons. They say her water's nice
and warm because volcano ventings stir
the bottom of her sea. I'm modestly
drinking *café au lait* at Borders. Sun
surprises with warm hands. The April tree
says *bloom.* I read the sunrays and have fun
with them. With sun it's not a crime to feel
glad for microbial life down in the black
waters of moons. We hunger for each bit
of life. Anywhere. I would crawl to steal
another second before life stops. The crack
in that moon's lake is sun. We're all sunlit.

Sun and I Are Outsiders

The sun and I are outsiders and far.
I'll die one night. The brain can't be replaced
like a bum heart or lung. Same as a car
you take down to a shop, bad parts erased
for new ones. The sun star can never die
or live because he has no DNA or skin
and blood. So we're a pair. His yellow eye
keeps me in shape for life. My eyes have been
his scribe for good, giving him press and maps,
some names and history. And we're closer still.
The sun is my dark night of love. I wake
in his red arms, cloudy or not. He wraps
me in his light (my moon's a frozen hill)
and float in dream up to his burning lake.

Stillness in the Sun

Let me sit in the sun. Sun doesn't cure
all ills (only time does) but the gas star
heats us with calm. The Bosnians still endure
the club of greed. Wilfred Owen, not far
from his young death, wrote, *Move him in
the sun—the amputee in his chair.* I need
to know the breeze of peace again. I've been
an actor who cannot sit still, and feed
my nervous fears by showing pages of
a sketchpad or a manuscript to friends.
If they approve I glow a while. The sun
is blind and stands outside in massive love
for earth. Unhurried doves ascend. I run
for life. Am still in sun. Burning it mends.

Dante
Awoke in
Hell and
You Came
Thin on
Morning
Hills

Dante Awoke in Hell and You Came Thin on Morning Hills

Comrade sun, why aren't you well behaved
like a calm moon who's stormy once in a
green moon? Your gas explodes. I'm saved
from malice by averting your death ray
of flame into my eye. The waters gleam
next to Longfellow Bridge and almost nude
joggers and cyclists soak you up. I *seem*
to be a while. You *are.* My solitude
longs for your public party face. Don't talk.
Hugging me with your boiling arms feels good
enough. Dante awoke in Hell and you
came thin on morning hills. In my black wood
of death, you'll laugh at my dim state. This walk
in Boston (where my dad saw light) will do.

Sun, Don't Let Me Down

> *... the plow blade touches the flower at the field's edge ...*
> — *Catullus*

I am a wise guy sometimes. It's a bluff.
Crossing the streets, under your watch, I gulp
and sigh. I'm sentimental and it's rough
to know you'll read this mushy inky pulp
in a computer book when I am gone,
when you, bright sun, have learned your ABCs.
Why do I grieve? A habit? I've withdrawn
to hear Catullus moan on shaking knees:
*When our brief sun has set, our life will be
a never ending sleep.* The truth is sick.
I can't control the clock yet can be now,
which is eternal anyway, and trick
my heart to feel the sun in Greece. I see
us fall, the poppy's throat nicked by the plow.

Qaddafi's Fresh Sunny Shirt

for Khaled Mattawa

Khaled tells me about his Tripoli
and the ancient sun Phoenicians wrap in parch-
ment and—still hot—dump on the Libyan Sea
where, washing slowly to a Roman arch
over the beach, it lights his mom's backyard.
Her young cousin Qaddafi is proud, lean,
hanging out in the kitchen and quite hard
up. He needs a good coat, nice cuisine,
and a fresh white shirt to wear in the sun
before making a revolution. "Give
the guy some figs, couscous, take him outside,
and scrub away the lice," Mom says. With gun
and sunny shirt, he's sure not to forgive
the king or skip a bloody regicide.

Sun Coloring Boston

On the walls in Boston in the Museum
of Fine Arts, Matisse is painting lemon sunshine
and loving blue. Chagall is painting dream.
Through the glass ceiling the sun drops a line
of fire across the floor on which I dance
dizzy and sore before that hammer star
who bops me out of time. Now in a trance
I feel his sunstroke rays frying a scar
of history through my fuzzy hatless brain.
On the frontier Anne Bradstreet in her room
wrote sun into a dying child. Her pen,
stronger than fire burning her house, makes pain
Emily-sharp. An artist's room stops time.
Boston. I watch Monet's light on the Seine.

Dining on French Moon and Drinking Boston Sun

A Paradise that resembles the Vatican is my idea of Hell.
— Jorge Luis Borges

When I was young death was concept, a tool
for church and synagogue to terrorize
and promise paradise. I was no fool
and knew that nature inflicts its dim prize
of nothingness. I have survived TB,
old-fashioned killer. Now death's not abstract.
Only in *now* comes flash eternity.
There is no show-time after the last act.
With six lines left there's nothing good to say
except I am the same age as our Pope,
feel and look better than morose Ben,
who offers sky-blue heaven and faith hope.
I dine on moon, drink sun and know my end.
Like a tramp I love light and hear grass pray.

Van Gogh's Sun

At George School I buy three cheap Van Gogh prints
and send them to my father who frames them
in Colorado. They watch his footprints
next to the iron stairs. The sunflower stem
holds Vincent's burning eyes seizing a vision
of Provence, pigments, Gauguin, horrid sale
no fame. When dad stops being the magician
from Mexico, he walks to the black rail,
leaps from the roof and floats like black sun
down to the bloody street. On his office walls
I find Van Goghs. I know he hung them there
for me. I'm getting off the sub. Boston.
Climbing the museum stairs where Van Gogh calls
me to reclaim the sun and father's air.

Saint John of the Cross Soars into the Sun

Saint John of the Cross soars into the sun
in his dark night. He sees his lover's face
where no one seems to be. Oblivion
and ecstasy. He sleeps on her. No place,
no time until they wake among the lilies.
Father in his black noon loses his love
of day. The phone terrifies him. Achilles
hugs a vague shade in hell, a phantom of
his father gone forever. When dad steps
into the dark, like John, he doesn't go
away. We bury him. I can't keep track,
however, since his love haunts me. In snow
high in Tibet we climb the sun. We trek
Nepal. When I am bushed he takes my pack.

Happiness of the Patient Traveler

I write a letter to the sun
to shine on us again for one
more life. Then beg him for the time
to let our tongues agree to rhyme
for one more year. And then I ask
for just a day, but he unmasks
me with the alphabet of night,
and when I plead for still more light
he spits on me with hours of rain
which finally washes out the pain
of time. I write a letter to
the sun and say I shall let go
of love. He leads me to a tree
inside, where I will hang and be.

Sun, If I Died

Sun, if I died would you still want to live?
My wife said she would not. She's wrong, but mad-
ly loyal. You have a world of light to give
and have no choice. Would you feel bad or glad
or anything? I love you. How can you
be such a shit? We're friends. When you were young
in Egypt like a golden scarab, blue
Pharaohs shaped you like them, a god. They hung
you on their chest. We feed you heart blood in
Mesoamerica. Girls burn their buns
for looks with your old hand in risky play.
You give us life, but I want more. You win.
We fake you human, but your soaring tons
of hot indifference coldly create day.

My Father Sun of Romantic Days

My father sun, my father who's not here
(and most of childhood was not), now each place
we live together, walk to, is a near
collision of red happiness. Your face
persists in Mexico, on gray Broadway,
on speedy deserts of the patient West
in our white Buick. What romantics! Play
and work. War year. Dames and sun. In your vest
you keep a bag of diamonds. From them come
our bread and costs of love. Pour them on blue
velvet and change them magically to green-
backs. Texas night is endless. We become
a long white moon, smash a deer's ass, and you
and I drive till sun lifts sweetly and obscene.

Dancing with the Sun

The wind is dancing tango with the wind
at midnight. Rats are waltzing under streets.
The river leopard has the cosmos pinned
to infant pepper trees while in my sheets
death is the darkest room to contemplate,
no shadow of the shadow. Wonder why
such pain when pain is gone, when on that date
unknowable there is no hell, nor cry
of heaven. Crude Lucretius said, *Why fear
what is the end of fear?* There is no wrong
or right way out of being. I don't expect
to dance when I am dead. You'll be my song,
my sun and partner while we trip a perfect
tango with wind I love and cannot hear.

Time Is a Ferryboat Lumbering One Way

Time is a ferryboat lumbering one way
for each of us, yet floating endlessly,
porting new customers for a quick lay.
Shakespeare in sonnets cursed the husbandry
of hideous time which, cultivating death,
defaces us. Yet ferries hold their course,
ferrying you, allowing me a breath
of life, until we drown below the floors
of rock where no time shines. I wonder how
I've lasted while the young collapse. William
himself died young but not before he got
his feather pen to decorate a bough
with wrinkled suns against the cold. I am
his ship of wormy time, blessing his rot.

After Oppenheimer Knew His Sunbomb Worked

We have known sin, Rob Oppenheimer[10] said
after he knew his sunbomb worked. It brought
a bit of photosphere to earth. The dead
light up like sunlight. Hiroshima is hot,
a tiny star pinned on the earth. It weeps,
its star goes out, but radium holds it live
till all the dead have died. The big sun keeps
exploding and the killing fields survive
and glitter. Oppenheimer soon is hit
and dies as if he too were burned by Hell.
There are no moral executions. When
the electric chair works like a hypocrite
to sun a criminal, the graveyards yell
with every shot of flame, *Never again!*

Sunflower

Yellow moon mirror of the sky's fire rock,
you turn your head to your own colored sun
and measure dawn and dayfall like the clock
of heaven till the dead clock's work is done.
At night you cannot dream, although you grow,
alive unlike your sun twin in the sky.
A plant and gaseous rock, a bride and beau,
a stunning pair, beauty and wonder, the eye
of day and leaf of time, you speak the light
of silence. Both of you are mute. I'm glad
to be your talking friend. That's all I do,
talk and record. But you don't long to right
or wrong the world. You add. One night you clad
China in sunflowers concealed in dew.

Childhood

Sun has a thousand faces. The steel choir
of Brooklyn Bridge looks over Maiden Lane,
her milkmaid alleys shaded from his fire
most of the day. High buildings. Commerce. Gain
or bankruptcy. We drop a nickel in
the slot and tunnel from the West Side down
to Chambers Street. You read *The Sun.* The din
and clatter stills till we climb up John
Street to cool light. We stroll in sunfun past
Pildes. I climb a lamppost. You are proud
of us and Pierre Grange watches, your design.
Then one night we go broke. We have a blast
uptown, lodged in a bad hotel on loud
Broadway, and pan for sun in our goldmine.

Into May Sun, 1946

You are a self-made man, but you made me
and still make me, though you went long ago.
You have some cash left—for say two cups of tea
and a quick passage down to Mexico,
a futile one. I come down from Maine. We walk
the pavements of New York and do not sleep
this night, our last one. All night long we talk
and it is grand and bad. The dawn comes deep
with worry. You, broken, batter my heart.
I go back north, we talk once more. The call
is bad. I cannot come. You fly off to
the south. The sun declines to rise. His art
of pleasure doesn't show. You jump and all
we are is sun. Sun with me even now.

Buddha

The Buddha sitting on the sun is not
proselytizing but taking a nap.
Earlier, seeking enlightenment, the thought
of his dear wife and child, the palace trap
of comfort almost breaks his will to dump
them all, but gods turn earth around so he
looks straight ahead. Siddhartha, now grown plump
with canny vision under the Bodhi Tree,
lays his new holiness on sumptuous sun.
The earth grows dark in spots, a fine eclipse
for voyeurs. When the sun drops to his knees,
the Buddha in his mythic pose is done
with light. Poisoned by meat, death on his lips,
as a bronze statue filled with light he flees.

Jesus Nailed in the Sun

Jesus the rabbi is nailed on the cross
by occupying Romans. Last sun. But
he doesn't know he isn't human. Loss
of life is agony and big spikes cut
his feet and hands in unbearable pain,
but he is just a Jew who Romans said
was trouble. Pilate takes the role of Cain
murdering the Semite so he'll be dead
without his blessing or his sheep. At noon
they nail the rebel. Now he cannot leak
in public: Yeshua's the Mashiah, friends
whisper. He doesn't know it, or why Greek
will be his cover name and tongue. He ends
on fire. The night sun fails. Black is the moon.

Car Ferry in Northern Vermont

The car's up front. Overhead, gossipy birds
worry about the ferry in the sun.
Destiny East. I've spent my life on words
although below the sea the words are gone.
Slowly the talk, friends, love born on a hill
become a haze of gulls. Way back. The sky
below the sea is closed even to Gilgamesh
who cannot undo death. To die
is nature, but the boat is ticking on
into the sun. It's WHITE out there. Sun white!
and our few hours elect eternity
until we dock down in the carless night
below. I sigh for love lost in the sea
although below the sea the dark is gone.

Sun Is Filled with Oranges

> *Quiero escribir, pero me sale espuma.*
> *I want to write, but foam comes out.*
> —César Vallejo

I love to meditate upon the sun
and moon, the pleasure of the mango, and
sometimes by scribbling I compound the fun,
my habit, while I scoop up lunar sand
for the Great Wall of China that I set
in Bosnia for safekeeping. Sun is filled
with oranges first painted in Tibet,
blood oranges whose memory chilled
with mountain gods and murder. In a daze
of sweet escape through awful dark to light,
from moon and sun, I toss my aching head
off a Peloponnesian cliff. To laze
with words left over from the fall, I write
these lies by someone bright and moon-sun dead.

Snow Killed Osip Mandelstam

Osip Mandelstam was right. He understood
the artist in his day was worthy of
being shot; even under the Czar could
be picked up as a conscience, jailed above
the Arctic Circle, yet survive as soul
to starved readers. Snow killed Osip—no love
for martyrdom. Anna Akhmatova and Osip
memorized each other's poems
(memory was their computer disk
of survival in years of tyranny).
He wasn't shot. Sick,
shoveling ice in a pack of prisoners,
he collapsed. Osip was a great ghost
of battered brain juggling words till he cracked.

Miguel de Unamuno's Midnight Sun

In Spain Miguel de Unamuno at
his desk turns out another desperate tale.
It's midnight and the desk is old and splattered
with ink like his hero Manuel
the Good who is a priest and can't believe
in oak trees or a sky with God. The Basque
cranky writer is cold. His grim black sleeve
contains a smaller book. Through it he'd bask
in midnight sun, yet night gives little hope
of cutting loose from tragic sense. He and
his hero—a godless Spaniard fencing death—
want everlasting sun. He has a loupe
to study clues. He pokes below the sand
of darkness for eternal sun and breath.

Dream

Below

the

Sun

Dream Below the Sun

Why wake to awareness of illusion? Dream,
the normal state, lets time below the sun
perform its act of slipping speech, daydream
and daybeams into our mind like someone
controlling things. The truth of emptiness
is much too painful. Once, I saw the void,
looked in and slipped endlessly down. The mess
of absence is a boring long tabloid,
screaming: *You are nowhere, no one!* My friend
Antonio Machado knows the blur.
I watch his landscapes dream. Interior sky
fills him. In him mountains of Soria send
their snowy backs robed in the sun's white fur.
A sunning bull is better than night's lie.

Antonio's Blue Days and Childhood Sun[11]

Machado has a small room on the Street
of the Abandoned Children in Segovia.
He writes on a table, warming his feet
from a brazier below. Andrés Segovia
in the casino's smoky parlor plays
Falla. Below the teacher's kitchen window
a tiny monastery grave displays
the tomb of Juan de la Cruz; there grow
lilies by the dovecot. Antonio, poet
walking afternoon roads alone, commends
his gaze to storks on belfries. War expels
and he escapes to France over fierce hills
of February slop and snow. He ends
his walk, a blue day of sun in his pocket.

Sun Became Black like Sackcloth of Hair

from Revelation 6 (Apocalypse)

When the lamb opened the sixth seal I looked
and there took place a great earthquake
and the sun became black like sackcloth of hair
and the full moon became like blood,
and the stars of the sky fell to the earth
as the fig tree dropped its unripe fruit
shaken by a great wind. And the sky
vanished like a scroll rolling up,
and every mountain and island of the earth
was torn up from its place and moved.
And the kings of the earth and the great men
and commanders of thousands and every slave
and the free hid in caves and mountain rocks,
and said to the mountains and rocks, Fall on us
and hide us from the face of him who is sitting
on the throne and from the anger of the lamb
because the great day of his anger has come,
and before him who has the force to stand?

Letter to Baruch Spinoza

I pen a letter to my lord
Spinoza. His way has no end.
More than his lumpy Latin word,
his reasoned thought forever lends
me consolation. God is all,
is nothing. Pantheist God is sun,
and the glass dust that makes him fall
at forty-four. No groan, no gun
of doubt deflects him from the calm
of his transcendence. A comrade
in TB, he foods on love, his hand
holds circus feats of time, his palm
guards planets, rain, and a good land
where cosmic light protects the sad.

The Man of Glass

Will you stick with me, sun? I'm made of glass
and you shine through. You shine and I'm alive.
At night I sleep because I know you'll pass
through me again. I need light to survive
above the ground. I'm not a man of gloom,
a downer. Ask my friends. But I'm not well
these days, and locked inside a steamy room,
wanting the sun and not to crack, I smell
the fall. It's long and lovely in this state.
Maybe I am a gloom grub, yet one chance
to eat a watermelon in Kashgar
and I am gone, the gypsy. My odd fate
is nature designated me to dance
the role of me. I'm glass and focus far.

Mystics Convert Darkness into Night Sun

In my dark room I see the sun. It's right
and natural. Sun is in the mind. That's where
it is, even outside. I watch the light
this morning cooling Indiana air
here in the woods, on yellow poplar, oak
(my barn is made of it) and slender beech.
Though ignorant of nature, who will choke
my air to death, I relish her green speech,
her sometime calm. In my dark room the sun
permits me hope. Sees me voyage. My books
are sun because they convert darkness in-
to an amateur's blazing night and stun
the fear of dying. Night sun like mountain brooks
sparkles and I laugh lost in her cool inn.

Living Alone with the Unknown

To live alone at my age is to be
a Quietist, Miguel de Molinos.
I eat my books for breakfast and drink tea
called Morning Thunder. Quiet and the φως—
Greek light—I dream them both. While in a chair
right out of bed I talk out loud, hoping
to look through bone and loaf in frozen air.
All this weirdness is proper Spanish being.
I love what I am not, the mystic Juan
of nothingness who carries sun at night
to walk to unseen love. He was alone,
a woman pierced by God. I haven't gone
to sleep again, and look, there is no light
inside. I live alone with the unknown.

Gobbling the Sun While Reading My Obit

On the first lazy day of spring I loaf
outside and sit an hour, gobbling the sun
for breakfast. Then pull out the *Times.* An oaf
I skim, and spot my obit. It is fun
to have the chance to read about the death
of me, WB. It isn't cruel:
A young professor killed. I check my breath.
At least it wasn't suicide. The fool
drowned in a tub. The rest is silence—just
the overflow—and yet the silence kills
me twice; I've lost all greed for readership.
Saint Paul phones me. It helps. He says he'll bust
me in the jaw for my mistakes. I fill
my glass with words. The tub utters drip, drip.

Piano on the Sun

I take my piano to the sun and play
with night. I play Chopin. The sun might fail
to rise, he's so romantic. Then the Milky Way
draws near. It listens jealously. A whale
pulls up in minor C so he can hear and squirts
his fountain in applause. O sun, we two
have mesmerized both art and universe.
Pythagoras loved star songs in the blue
of evening. He hears us. Apollinaire
(who's even crazier) gets in a truck
and carts a ton of smoking crêpes straight up
to our lips. A poet's way. Playing an air
from Spain, I dance all night with moon. My cup
is full. Sun burns the feet of my good luck.

Plain Love Poem to You and Sun

To say plain things I need a metaphor.
Ecclesiastes says: The sun also
rises and the sun also sets. Before
he hits Jerusalem, Yeshua ben Yosef
asks to save a room on the second floor
where he and his students will meet and grow
their night of nights with bread and wine, and word
his metaphor of body, blood, and mind.
In Songs the lovers hear the turtledove
singing across the land. The cuckoo bird
and gazelle thrive on sands of war and love.
I wear a ring. I take it off at night;
miss it. You are in darkness, breathing light,
and when we wake the sun comes through the blind.

Sun, Be More Than a Train Watcher While the Cattle Cars Roll By

These nights I wonder. Older, I have read
Emily Dickinson amazing the page, her soul
annihilated by Calvinist God
who doesn't elect her. You glow her whole
in white through bedroom curtains. You have
her ecstasies and death. You know us all.
You know my father too. I see him lean
on you one afternoon next to a wall
in Taxco. His bald pate a gold peso
mirroring glorious escape. You watch him die.
He flies through you. And every morning I
have left, you boom, I am your father and
the holy sun. Reading your stunning O,
I chill before your flaming heart of sand.

Gas Lamp, 1893

In brownstone Boston down on old Milk Street,
up two gray flights, near the gas lamp, the tailor
waits glumly for the midwife. August heat
has worn the woman out. Amid the squalor
she looks around the bed, clutching a cape
she brought from London as a child. It's dawn
and dirty. The dark tailor wants to escape
to his cramped shop. The woman's sheets are drawn
below her waist. She isn't hollering now.
Her eyes are dark and still; blood on her thumbs.
Her name is Sarah. No. I'm guessing. How,
untold, am I to know? Pale sun has worn
into the room. The midwife finally comes.
Grandmother bleeds to death. My father's born.

We Drive Down into Mexico; in Colorado You Dive into Sun

You drive to Colorado, a young state,
you write me, where a person says hello
to you on any morning in the street.
It is a shock, that friendliness. To go
with strangers and feel good. You teach me how
to drive, we race all night till dawn and come
to Amarillo and Laredo. Young hot cow-
boys flashing into Mexico. Your name
is written on a grave in '46,
stone letters for your earthly sign. Father,
you never can get old like me, because
you choose to float down wingless and to mix
your bones with blasting sun. I cannot pause
because I'm chasing you, the youth we are.

He Was Younger Than Sun

The afternoon my father died
I got a call. The act was done
and never done. I cried and cried
and he was younger than the sun.
Since then, the first death I would know,
time is insane. The fall of Constantinople
is still a blow
today, and though I am not gone
I worry as if it has occurred
already. Maybe it helps that years
confound inside. It's less absurd
than measured separation. Time
is young. My father sighs. His ears
once scarred, he listens for my rhyme.

Stand Up Tall and Be Happy

Sweet dad, you always say to stand up tall.
It makes me happy. We are walking on
a street in Colorado, a sweet fall
before your leap. In August the huge bomb
cremates Hiroshima and the long war
is gone. An afternoon in Mexico
at our Quaker peace camp, the radio
suddenly reports the sun explodes. Whore
of Babylon. That fall the demons sleep.
We have, as always, just a few good days
and then I wander East. If you were live,
what would I be? More confident? Your grace
is bright. A poet? After your leap I weep
and learn the night. Your tall sun has survived.

Give Me Another Mile with You

I'm sorry for you, father. Now I know
the belt of fire you wore. I feel it too.
Your demons had you reeling. I can go
another mile. You couldn't make it through
another day and flew into the sun
and darkness. And from pain and light you're free.
I hurt and worry but I'm not yet done
with words and love. You'd be 103
today if you were sitting with me here
alone as you were when you took the stair
up to the roof, the narrow path to death.
Too young. Now I'm your older brother. Stare
at me out of your horror pit nowhere.
I love you. Help me taste each lucky breath.

The Prodigal Son (Luke 15:11–32)

We are two sons. Father gives me my share
of wealth and soon I gather a few clothes
and books and take a ship into the glare
of Paris where I spend my loot on booze
and women; and one night of revelry
I got so stoned a thief comes to my room,
bags everything I own in sheets. With glee
he taps downstairs and flees. I feel no gloom
and never write my folks until I starve
in Spain. By then my father dies, and I
come back to search for him. He sees me far
away from where he lies and calls, *I've carved
a cloud in here for you.* "Make me your slave,"
I groan. "I've sinned. Take me from sun." But he
says, *You my child were dead and now you are
alive.* He drinks my tears washing his grave.

Be Gentle, Sun

Be gentle, sun. You know no end.
I do. Your memory has a bil-
lion parts. I ask my gentle friend
for time below the sun. The thrill
of light. Or dark of madness or
disease. It matters, but as long
as you persist in me and soar
at dawn, our pact is good. I'm wrong
to ask you, gentle sun. But I
can't choose my love. I came. You were
and are and will be. Dig me deep
with all the light from your glass eye.
Be gentle, sun. I want to sleep
yet also wake. In me occur.

Gem Stones

Although my father is a jeweler, and pop
could spot the sun inside a rock, and gave
me New York afternoons of roaming store
to store with him to make some dough, my grave
will store these bones as cheap barn stones, not gems.
Dad's eyes were beryl and he wore a pearl
stickpin in a silk tie until the Thames
froze over and he groped for warmth. His girl
in Mexico went cold. He jumped, but in
his tomb the walls were live. I heard his moans,
his nails scratching to climb to sun. I said,
"I'll dig you out," and find a secret inn
in blue Bolivia where he seems not dead.
There dad and I share gem light, we poor stones.

My Father First Saw the Sun on Milk Street

Each child tumbling out on the grass of life—
like the guanaco born in Patagonia—
sees sun, is innocent, and then the knife
cuts free the mother's cord till her pneumonia
drops that child in dark. My father saw
the sun on Milk Street, though his mother paid
his birth with death. Some of us fall to law
of ovens like the spinning lily made
to live a day and then be cast to fire,
and some feel guilt for having kept our sun
alive. I'm innocent, and yet I hurt
since one I loved tumbled from the high wire
between two roofs and bloodied his fresh shirt.
He's here with me, trying to greet his son.

Love Tent

Every few years I dig around and find
a letter from my father with the seal
of some hotel he stopped at, going blind-
ly town to town to make himself a deal
and work his way again back up on top.
It's far ago. I'm just like him. I try
to make time work for me, but time the cop
of death will cuff me as he nabbed him. I'll sigh
and go. The sun on that black Monday will
forget to rise, I'll be holed up in bed
yet scrawl a letter back to him. Dad went
except in me. He takes my hand. I fill
his palm of dust with sun. And we're not dead
because we love and chat in his blue tent.

Afterchat

After years of dryness, in February 1922 Rainer Maria Rilke wrote his *Sonnets to Orpheus* in the first four days of an extraordinary twenty-two days of creation. He wrote most of the *Duino Elegies* in those same weeks. That spell, that dictation where one is scribe to a voice and tune, was always my desire. I had just finished translating *Sonnets to Orpheus,* and I don't recall what led me to meditate on the sun and moon, but once I started, Rilke's twenty-two days were the measure (add fifteen years of revisions and additions). It was silly and arbitrary, but one July it got me through *Sunbook.* Then in August came *Moonbook,* composed by the same measure. All this happened in Boston. My father was born on Milk Street in Boston in 1893, and the meditation soon centered on him, whose life and death have shaped much of my life. I was his son, he was my sun, and I learned, through his early violent death, what it meant for the sun to set yet persist even now.

Café Annastassi
Le Palais Royal, Paris
2013

Notes

1 "Gospel of Clouds" (page 2):

The *peat bog soldiers* were prisoners of war in the Börgerniir Nazi concentration camp in Lower Saxony. The song was composed in German by inmates and sung by thousands of inmates as they marched with their digging spades instead of rifles. It became a resistance song in many languages during World War II. In his resonant voice Paul Robeson famously sang it both in German and in English.

Wir sind die Moorsoldaten
und ziehen mit dem Spaten ins Moor.
Wir sind die Moorsoldaten
und ziehen mit dem Spaten ins Moor.

We are the peat bog soldiers,
Marching with our spades to the moor.
We are the peat bog soldiers,
Marching with our spades to the moor.

2 "Poètes dans la lune" / "Poets in the Moon" (page 14):

Written originally in French, then translated into English in Café de l'Aube à Paris (the Dawn Café, in Paris).

3 Working in Talks Around Midnight" (page15):

José López Rega, minister of police (1974–1976) under Argentinian president Isabelita Perón, who was his lover. He headed the infamous AAA, which murdered at least 1,500 people during his reign. *"El brujo"* means "male witch."

4 "Lune à Paris, 1948" / "Moon in Paris, 1948" (page 21):

Written originally in French, then translated into English for Café Apollinaire à Paris.

5 "Max Jacob the Day He Was Seized" (page 22):

Max Jacob is punning on the similarity in sound in French of *Gestapo* and *J'ai ta peau.* The French G before a vowel is pronounced as a soft g like the consonant *j*.

6 Dylan Looks Great, 1953" (page 29):

Saint Vincent's, the Greenwich Village hospital in New York where Dylan Thomas died on November 9, 1953.

7 "Old Orchard Plane and a Sad Black Moon, 1933" (page 36):

In his poem "Dark Night of the Soul," Saint John of the Cross (San Juan de la Cruz, 1542) ascends and descends in the sky.

8 "Dancing Greek with Kerouac Until Dawn's Sun" (page 50):
With the phrase *Nel mezzo del cammin* ("Midway on the road") begins the first line of
Canto 1 of Dante's *Inferno* in the *Comedia.*

9 "Sun Rises and Ceases to Shine" (page 58):
Kohelet or Qohélet ("gatherer" in Hebrew) is the philosophic preacher of earthly vanity
in Ecclesiastes. The title of Hemingway's novel *The Sun Also Rises* is from Ecclesiastes 4,
"The sun also rises and the sun goes down."

10 "After Oppenheimer Knew His Sunbomb Worked" (page 78):
Robert Oppenheimer cited the *Bhagavad-Gita,* saying, "Now I am become Death, the
destroyer of worlds."

11 "Antonio's Blue Days and Childhood Sun" (page 84):
Antonio Machado died in Collioure, France, on February 22, 1939. His last composed
verse was found in his pocket and reads, *Estos días azules y este sol de la infancia:* "These
blue days and this sun of childhood," referring to his childhood in Sevilla.

Acknowledgments

Some of these poems have previously appeared in the following books and periodicals:

Algebra of Night: New & Selected Poems 1948–1998 (Sheep Meadow Press, 1998), *The American Scholar, The Antioch Review, Borges at Eighty: Conversations* (New Directions, 2013), *Café de l'Aube à Paris / Dawn Café in Paris* (Sheep Meadow Press, 2011), *Chicago Review, Cut-Bank, The Dream Below the Sun: Selected Poems of Antonio Machado* (Crossing Press, 1981), *Five A.M. in Beijing: Poems of China* (Sheep Meadow Press, 1987), *The Formalist, Holiday Magazine, Kayak, The Kenyon Review, Lifewatch, The Massachusetts Review, The New Republic, New Letters, The New Yorker, Nimrod, The Secret Reader: 501 Sonnets* (University Press of New England, 1996), *Saturday Evening Post, Six Masters of the Spanish Sonnet* (Southern Illinois University Press, 1997), *Southern Review, The Sewanee Review,* and the *Times Literary Supplement.*

Other books from Tupelo Press

Fasting for Ramadan: Notes from a Spiritual Practice (memoir), Kazim Ali
Another English: Anglophone Poems from Around the World,
     edited by Catherine Barnett and Tiphanie Yanique
Circle's Apprentice (poems), Dan Beachy-Quick
The Vital System (poems), CM Burroughs
Stone Lyre: Poems of René Char, translated by Nancy Naomi Carlson
Severance Songs (poems), Joshua Corey
New Cathay: Contemporary Chinese Poetry, edited by Ming Di
The Posthumous Affair (novel), James Friel
Into Daylight (poems), Jeffrey Harrison
Ay (poems), Joan Houlihan
Nothing Can Make Me Do This (novel), David Huddle
Darktown Follies (poems), Amaud Jamaul Johnson
Dancing in Odessa (poems), Ilya Kaminsky
A God in the House: Poets Talk About Faith (interviews),
   edited by Ilya Kaminsky and Katherine Towler
domina Un/blued (poems), Ruth Ellen Kocher
Phyla of Joy (poems), Karen An-hwei Lee
Engraved (poems), Anna George Meek
Boat (poems), Christopher Merrill
Body Thesaurus (poems), Jennifer Militello
Mary & the Giant Mechanism (poems), Mary Molinary
Lucky Fish (poems), Aimee Nezhukumatathil
Long Division (poems), Alan Michael Parker
Ex-Voto (poems), Adélia Prado, translated by Ellen Doré Watson
Intimate: An American Family Photo Album (memoir), Paisley Rekdal
Thrill-Bent (novel), Jan Richman
Vivarium (poetry), Natasha Sajé
Calendars of Fire (poems), Lee Sharkey
Cream of Kohlrabi: Stories, Floyd Skloot
Traffic with Macbeth (poetry), Larissa Szporluk
The Perfect Life (essays), Peter Stitt
Swallowing the Sea (essays), Lee Upton
Butch Geography (poems), Stacey Waite
Dogged Hearts (poems), Ellen Doré Watson

See our complete backlist at www.tupelopress.org